BROKEN PIECES MAKE THE PERFECT BUILDING BLOCKS

Healing From Betrayal

LaShawn Walker

Copyright © 2023 LaShawn Walker

ALL RIGHTS RESERVED. This book contains material protected under International and Federal Copyright Laws and Treaties. Any unauthorized reprint or use of this material is prohibited. No part of this book may be reproduced or transmitted in any form or by any means, electronic or mechanical, including photocopying, recording, or by any information storage and retrieval system without express written permission from the author/publisher.

Unless otherwise noted, all scripture quotations are taken from the King James Version of the Bible. All rights reserved.

Book Cover Design: Chelsea Nicholette Callender (Chelsaline.Studio) and Prize Publishing House

Printed by: Prize Publishing House, LLC in the United States of America.

First printing edition 2023.

Prize Publishing House
P.O. Box 9856, Chesapeake, VA 23321
www.PrizePublishingHouse.com

ISBN (Hardcover): 979-8-9884324-8-7
ISBN (E-Book): 979-8-9884324-9-4

Cover Credits

Photographer: Thomas Kirk
Instagram: @thomaskirk_
Website: http://www.thomaskirkphotos.com

Makeup Artist: FOLAKEMI Awelewa
Instagram: @beautyperfectionmakeover

Hair Stylist: Kyra Barnes
Instagram: @shopbeautebar

Nail Artist: Toi Swint
Instagram: @nailsbytoi

Fashion Stylist: Trendy & Praizey
www.trendyandpraizey.com

A NOTE FROM THE AUTHOR

Broken Pieces Make the Perfect Building Blocks encourages readers not to disregard life's events that may appear to be shattered due to loss of trust or, in some instances, betrayal. I see no need to suffer without a future that includes healing.

I was compelled to share my voice and story in hopes that it would be somewhat of a blueprint as to where to start a healing journey.

Broken Pieces Make the Perfect Building Blocks includes a portion of my experiences, steps I took to heal, poetry, and review points to check progress. At the completion, there is a planner to assist in business notes, money moves, stash cash, and a monthly quote of encouragement.

Betrayal is not the actual act that caused distress
in your life but the disbelief that
the betrayer is someone you trusted.

TABLE OF CONTENTS

Introduction 7

Chapter 1: Disbelief & Reality 14

Chapter 2: Elements (Components) Of The Heart 19

Chapter 3: Broken Pieces 24

Chapter 4: Shut Out The Noise 28

Chapter 5: Undercover Fear 33

Chapter 6: The Final Detox 38

Chapter 7: All Is Forgiven 42

Chapter 8: Completion - No Expectations Of Man 46

Chapter 9: Try New Things 51

Chapter 10: Happiness Is Priceless 54

Chapter 11: Love Again 122

References ....

INTRODUCTION

Where do I start without actually telling the entire story? I know my encounter with marital infidelity and betrayal will make a great juicy novel or an epic movie, but that's not my purpose for sharing a portion of my experience, story, and voice.

People encounter different forms of betrayal daily, but very few talk about it. Most are left alone to suffer in silence because they feel empty inside, ashamed, and less than. I am sharing some of my experiences and healing process in hopes that others will have a point of reference to realign their lives.

Broken Pieces Make the Perfect Building Blocks is designed to allow the person who was betrayed to gain total access to the healing power that rests within their soul. One will realize that they are more than capable of healing from the betrayal and also from the broken trust of their betrayer.

Healing will become the most influential tool, along with completely releasing any anger, hatred, resentment, bitterness, unforgiveness, etc. Understand these entities have a subtle way of disguising themselves. One must be able to identify and differentiate between healing and harboring negative feelings. Any welcoming relationship with these negative entities is a sure setback to an individual's healing progress. Now, let's begin to gather all of the leftover broken pieces that appear to be shattered and dysfunctional. Well, let me just say building a life of unfamiliarity will become an open book to the start of newness.

CHAPTER 1

DISBELIEF & REALITY

The marital infidelity was over a series of eight months. As I began to pay close attention to the changes in my spouse of 12 years, I was in total disbelief. I remember not wanting to face reality. But how could I not? Betrayal was all around me. Regardless of the constant denial, deep down in my spirit, I knew the truth. My spirit and natural man went back and forth. One day, praying for hours, and the next day, shedding tears, asking myself how this could be happening. Despite how or why, I had to find a way to function with a broken heart. I held my head high, not allowing anyone but my unit (prayer partners) and God to see my brokenness.

Most days, the betrayal seemed to be out of control. It was almost as if it was a taunting game of disrespect. But, I refused to stoop low. I quoted God's word often. I told myself, "Eagles fly high, pigeons fly low" (Miles Munroe). You are a Queen, not a peasant, girl. I wrote unrhyming poems to comfort my soul. Love was keeping me hopeful. Love is God-ordained, which is what I allowed to be embedded in my mind.

Before the affair, we were what most would consider a happy, loving couple. Don't misunderstand me; we had our share of disagreements, but nothing too deep that we couldn't resolve.

Both of us were extremely spontaneous and loved to entertain. Dinner game parties were our favorite. It didn't matter the occasion; however, most people we associated with knew that the party would be at our house if we were in town. Oddly, each party would always end with us talking about God and spiritual things. This was the life we built together, and everyone knew it. When there were no people around, we enjoyed each other's presence. We always found each other fun; therefore, we could hang out all day and not get tired of each other.

He loved writing music, wrestling, and playing video games. I loved making jewelry, exercising, and trying new recipes. And we both loved God and watching movies. Although he rarely let me pick the movie, I watched it with him anyway. His excuse was that I always picked low-budget movies. Surprisingly, it was true. I would always have the same response, "I like to give everyone an opportunity." This was the fairness and the lawyer in me. I had this thing about being fair since I was about seven years old. I didn't like someone flexing and having what they thought was the upper hand over someone else. That stuck with me, so I was cautious about how I treated others.

We would often go out of town in the spare of a moment. On most holidays, we would take turns planning short trips. I remember before the disconnection, we spent my birthday (July) in Scottsdale, Arizona. We spent his birthday and our anniversary (August) in Las Vegas, Nevada. We had guests over for Thanksgiving; for Christmas, we were in Atlantic City, New Jersey.

As the new year approached, we were in church and later had a few guests over for breakfast. Life wasn't bad, but of course, there was always room for improvement.

I remember times when he would have thought of something, and I would say it. He would respond, "I was just thinking that," and I would say, without fail, "I love when we do that." Then we both would laugh. Sometimes, we would say things simultaneously, ending with us both laughing again. He would respond, "I know you love when we do that."

There was no denying our connection to each other. We even had our inside jokes with our eye contact that no one knew what we were saying but us.

So yes, four or five months later, when our relationship began to change, I definitely felt the pull away. I approached him once or twice about the distance. He denied any changes. Therefore, I kept silent, observed, and prayed.

I knew that this season in our life was not only going to be natural but also spiritual.

The Bible clearly tells us in Ephesians 6:12 (KJV), "For we wrestle not against flesh and blood, but against principalities, against powers, against rulers of the darkness of this world, against spiritual wickedness in high places."

Knitted

She was an untold story, lost memories, the ending of a journey, broken promises, a grieving heart, a wandering mind; she was pieces & fragments. The beginning & ending. She is the conclusion of misplaced trust. She is he who damaged her soul. He is she who never told. They together are experiences and patches. Together, they are man and woman who seek to heal each other's soul. They are strangers. They are love after love. They are soulmates!

Knitted was the first poem of many. Writing was not only a way of expressing my emotions, but it was a form of healing. Each poem was the beginning or end of a stage, allowing me to understand where I was in life. Writing became a vital tool I used often. It allowed me to control my emotions. I was able to confront and deal with how I was feeling at that particular time. I became aware and in tune with myself. I was extremely honest and not willing to neglect what I was feeling (I like to refer to this as not living over your emotions).

After completing my morning routine, if I felt happy, sad, angry, or overwhelmed, I stopped and explored why. When realizing who or what I allowed to cause this emotion, I began to reason until I figured out how to conquer, dominate, subdue, and release my feelings. You see, I didn't just go through the day not knowing what triggered my feelings without obtaining clarity. I must admit knowing sometimes was hurtful, but it was also healing my soul. Knowing was forcing me to acknowledge the reality of betrayal and adultery. The reality was I didn't deserve to be publicly humiliated and embarrassed. I dealt with the realities of how my then-spouse displayed such a lack of loyalty with no care for the life we had established together. I realized that the lack of respect and love displayed was somewhat devastating to me.

I often thought there had to be a better way to end a marriage peacefully. But I guess he thought differently.

So, my then-spouse began to slander my name. I became the narrative for his F.B. live videos. I heard untrue statements concerning myself. This was hurtful to me but extremely entertaining to others. Most people knew the truth but were unwilling to stand up for righteousness. Although I had receipts (videos and text messages), I was not interested in defending myself naturally. I spoke very little, prayed, and prepared to mourn and start my healing process.

I knew I had to detach and reframe my life.

Healing provided the perfect opportunity to complete the last chapter of 12 years and start a new book.

The next few steps were difficult but necessary. I began to make myself less accessible to people. My circle became so small I could count on one hand who I associated with. I proceeded with caution but continued looking forward to a new beginning. I knew the road to healing would have a lot of ups and downs. However, I was willing to take the route and start the journey.

I needed some type of everyday assistance. So, I made what I like to call a healing manifestation board. This board fed my spirit each morning. I would pray and then read my board. This board reminded me of who I was despite how I felt. The only element each day was what I believed. I programmed myself to confess that I am fearfully and wonderfully made. My name LaShawn, in English, means God is gracious. In Hebrew, it means God is merciful, and on most social media platforms, my name is interpreted as most beautiful, sensual, and very intelligent woman.

Every day, I reminded myself of what my name meant. I was determined to fly high like the eagles. I refused to fly low, although I was not feeling my best some days, but low was not an option for me.

On days when I felt like I wouldn't make it, I sought out wise counsel. Some days, I talked, and some days, I just listened. Nevertheless, I was healing from what I would consider a devastating experience I would not want to happen to anyone. I knew it was not always the actual act but who caused the betrayal that hurt the most because that person was thought of as being so much more than that. The cuts were deep, but the healing ran deeper than the pain.

LaShawn's Healing Manifestation Board

Everyone's healing process will be different. I encourage all to start to explore options to heal and not just ways to forget the betrayal.

This would be a great time to create your own healing manifestation board.

Review Points

- ❖ Separate unbelief from reality.
- ❖ Conquer, dominate, and subdue.
- ❖ Confront and deal with your emotions.
- ❖ It's okay to let go of unhealthy situations.
- ❖ Accept and prepare for your healing process (use your healing tools).
- ❖ Invest time into building your spirit and character.

CHAPTER 2

ELEMENTS (COMPONENTS) OF THE HEART

Although I told myself it was time to reframe life, my heart was stuck. It took a while for my heart to agree with my spirit. My heart just couldn't comprehend the betrayal. It was a struggle that I had to face daily. My fairytale thoughts and actuality were constantly in a battle.

My heart was full of love and cherished treasures; therefore, it did not understand the lack of honesty, and it only referred to the pure ability to trust. But yet, trust had been broken. Did trust fail me, or did I fail trust? I put my trust in what my heart granted me access to. Sometimes, the intent of a man's heart is not always good. Therefore, the question is, who can understand the heart of man?

I learned a valuable lesson. Trust is frequently earned. Life is a balance, and I promised myself never to allow someone other than God to become involved in every aspect of my life. It's okay to share life; however, people become a part of each other's lives, not their entire life.

Fairytales for the Lost Soul

Mysteries and hidden treasures running through the depth of thy heart. Whirlwinds and storms trying to convince the mind that true love is not divine. Particles and pieces of the past influencing one's will to neglect trust. Eyes closed but yet wide open to protect, to guard, and to defend at all cause with no peace & no rest. Tired and weary, running in a panic. Tears streaming down thy cheeks, hitting the tip of thy chin. Thy hand quickly wiping thy face. The fingers pinching thy arm and imagining waking up from a dream. Calling and searching for refuge but finally realizing the truth of life was far more than a fairytale. Desperately picking up the pieces and promising oneself to live life like there is no tomorrow. To love like they have never been hurt. Trust like they have never been betrayed. Believe like they have no unbelief. Ensuring one stops to listen to the hidden treasures of thy soul while allowing healing to be written on the tables of the heart. Allow love to consume thy soul.

"Fairytales for the Lost Soul" forced me to deal with the life I had once known and also the life I was getting to know. It allowed me to see that what I had been blocking out of my mind actually still resided deep in my heart. "Fairytales for the Soul" was an eye-opener and wake-up call. What I had imagined was indeed the truth. No more deception. I was now on a mission to realign my spirit with God's will for my life. Restoring my very being to complete wholeness while lacking nothing. It was me or the betrayal. I chose me!

I had begun to face my betrayer and pick up the broken pieces of life. There is truly a time and season for everything under the sun. Was it my time to experience the uncomfortable stage of accepting the truth and starting a new life? A stage where time and pain were on my side. I could deal with time, but what would I profit from pain? Who would even invite pain into their life? Pain is one of those unexpected guests that shows up and doesn't quite know when to leave.

Time and time again, I found myself not just being angry with my betrayer but also being angry with pain. It was unnecessarily inflicted upon me. I knew there was a way to escape the pain and emotional devastation, but at what cost? At this point, I was not willing to trust the words or actions of the person who didn't think their selfish, fleshly act of lack of self-control would affect multiple areas of my life.

My betrayer didn't want to admit that their actions were less than integral, so they tried to cover up a series of events, creating fictional stories of our lives together.

They took the easy way out. My betrayer blamed me, their childhood, and everyone around us for their dishonesty.

Time

Time is the essence of life and the purity of innocence. Time is the distance between now and eternity. Time is living in the present but wishing to fast forward to the future

One's willingness not to reminisce on past memories cheats time. Recalculating used time unknowingly allows the past to frame the future. Eternity is forever, and the wait forces one to dwell in the now. Oh, how quick present time passes, such as lightning moving through the sky. Oh, how time changes, such as the sun setting as the moon begins to take its place. Somewhere in between time, the cloud releases rain, the flowers bloom, and the grass becomes green. Finally, eternity decides to allow one to see forever.

"Time" was written as evidence that everyone recovers and heals at their own pace. I couldn't allow myself to believe that time, without actively working, would heal the pain I had experienced. I set aside a method and even made a daily and sometimes weekly schedule focusing on healing and regrouping. Making a road map assisted me with pain management. Pain did not have the privilege of residing in every moment of my life. Control the controllable in life. I had become an aggressive, active participant in my wholeness. As stated before, I was and still am completely honest with myself. My suggestion to you is also the same: honesty.

Acknowledge your feelings, and don't mask them. Understand that pain may enter in one form but be released differently. For example, at some point, pain may have entered your life as a devastating event or a traumatizing situation; however, one day, pain may come out as anger and then on another day as depression. No matter how much pain tries to make its arrival, the sincere truth is it is imperative that you are committed and determined to conquer, dominate, and subdue the pain.

Regrouping allows you to focus on the determination and trust you have within you. Continue to tell yourself you have come too far and are not willing to have a setback. Regaining your strength is not optional; it's a must. Seek counsel from the wise. However you choose to schedule your healing, make sure you monitor your daily and weekly progress. Always keep in mind that your healing process is about you and only you. You may find that others will want you to just get over it but continue your healing process. Always allow yourself time to process your feelings. Take the time you need to respond to the pain and the hurt you are experiencing.

Pain

Disguised as an indication that one is still alive. Pain has deceived many.

Pain has caused most to throw in the towel. Pain has invaded the mind making one to believe that there is no ending. Pain causes one to adjust to its false suffering. It filtrates the heart, dims the soul, and numbs the feelings. Pain has taken credit for breath. Pain controls emotions. Pain believes if it's not present, there will be no gain. Pain puts itself in high demand. Pain searches for false love who seems to be fine with living sadly ever after. Pain had forgotten ever after doesn't exist without once upon a time. Ever after the tears dry, ever after reality takes the place of false perceptions, ever after the dust clears, ever after the rain stops pouring, and finally, ever after is no more. Pain becomes a mere indication that healing is nigh. Once upon a time, happily ever after knew pain would show up. Happily ever after held on to healing.

Healing became healed happily ever after.

Review Points

- Do not allow your heart to control the reality of betrayal.
- Time is urgent but doesn't heal pain on its own.
- Map out your healing.
- It's okay to feel and manage pain.
- Actively stay engaged and focus on regrouping.
- Seek only wise counsel.

CHAPTER 3

BROKEN PIECES

The marital affair was starting to take a toll on me. There were times when I knew I was making progress. But, there also in my face was my spouse and the other woman. He continued to use social media as a platform to drag my name and character through the mud. In the midst of this drama, my father passed away. Somehow, God granted me enough strength to officiate at my father's homegoing service.

So, yes, I was literally mourning two deaths. The natural death of my father and the physical and spiritual death of the marriage.

At this point, I had not told my family of my spouse's actions. I did not want to tarnish his character. After all, he was a man of the cloth. Too many souls were already at risk of being lost. And we still had not figured out what we were going to do with the church. But, I was ready and willing to relinquish the Elect Lady title and gracefully walk away because I didn't want to jeopardize anyone giving up on God or faith. Therefore, I took an oath of silence until the time was appropriate to release the truth.

I held on to faith and to the God that so loved the world He gave his only begotten Son, that whosoever believeth in Him should not perish, but have everlasting life (John 3:16).

What a powerful act of unconditional love.

I pressed on with all my might. I visualized being emotionally restored. I owed it to myself not to give up and to love again.

The Sound of LOVE

Listen to the soft whisper of My voice piercing your soul. Hear the music that dwells in the heart. Music of water flowing down a stream. Puddles of dew left from the morning fog. Misty evergreen branches with the aroma & smell of pine. The essence and fragrance of oils simmering, waiting to drench loose rose petals. Petals sprinkled upon a canvas that led to a secret pathway. A pathway with hidden desires, hidden treasures, and hidden emotions that are not willing to expose the true sound of love. Love has you imagining a perfect story of how life should be so divine, mystic & full of passion. Love blots out anger; love takes the place of me, myself, and I. Love has a sound only the pure in heart can hear. Love has a look that only eyes wide shut can see. Love is whispering I am with you. Love made a promise I will never leave you.

Love insisted I will protect & keep My hands upon you.

Love is not a stranger.

Love is whispering, "Listen to my voice, follow my lead, and I will bring you to the ending of the canvas."

I am love, and I will allow your heart to love.

Love, I say love.

It is no secret what the Bible says concerning love (charity). One can have several gifts, but they have nothing if they do not possess charity.

I allowed myself to focus on self-love and healing constantly. I accepted responsibility for myself and the things I could change. Once again, I didn't mask my pain. I dealt with it. I didn't cover up my hurt. I prayed and spoke out loud, encouraging and reassuring myself that I would be completely healed from the past. As I continued to work on redeveloping myself, how I saw and wrote the vision of my future became the main source of healing.

I knew myself more than anyone else besides God. Therefore, if I felt like I wanted to laugh, scream, or cry, I did. As a matter of fact, I recall that during July - October 2020, not a day went by without me crying.

As time passed, so did the healing, but at a slower pace than I expected.

I wanted to rush healing. I wanted the pain of betrayal to disappear. I didn't want any traces of the marital affair that I was forced to experience. This time, I found myself not associating with anyone who knew what was and had happened. My circle became a short, thin line.

I became ghosted, off-grid, less accessible than ever before, and only found when I wanted to be found. This allowed my mind to rest and to be at peace.

I often sat and thought about how I perceived honesty and loyalty. It took me a while to comprehend that everyone's perception is different. Each person has a right to view life and situations how they see fit. It really doesn't matter who you are or what title you carry; it has and always will be one's free will to live the life they have created. The God's honest truth is simple: one has been given free will. They will do as they choose.

I continued to accept full responsibility for picking up the broken pieces of what was left of my shattered life.

I totally believed God was allowing me to regroup. So, I made it my business to work on my total being.

I tucked my wings and soared through the storm.

Yes, I said tucked. You see, when eagles face a storm, they don't fight against it. Eagles simply drop their wings and fold them beneath their bodies. Their wings assume a collapse position. This position helps them avoid extreme loads. Yes, tucking promotes less pressure when soaring through turbulence.

At this point, I was trying to reposition my life. The least amount of pressure, the better. Less pressure allowed me to make several wise decisions concerning my next move in life.

Oh, it wasn't easy. It was like playing UNO. I threw a skip and made it through the entire week with peace. Then the enemy threw out a draw two, and I was hit with more than one situation at a time. No worries, God was and is still with me. The ball was in my court. Excuse me; it's my turn! Draw four. I didn't fall for any distractions. My ears were not tuned to ungodly advice or people's opinions, and before I knew it, the month was over. I began to see some light, but not enough to let my guard down.

I tried not to do a lot of exposing others. I knew the truth would come out someday. Besides, the truth always outweighs a lie.

I asked God to allow me to walk in grace. I continued to seek counsel while preparing for what I thought would be the next stage in life. I decided to be by myself and dedicate one year to healing. Advancing forward, I wanted to ensure that there were no trigger points I had not dealt with. I wanted to enjoy life at its finest.

I still believe somewhere out there that honesty, faithfulness, integrity, and love exist. Thou shalt receive all life has to offer. Therefore, the best advice I could give anyone is to heal completely. Do not leave any damaged area untouched. Life is waiting on you.

Review Points

- ❖ Reevaluate becoming less accessible (dedicate time for you).
- ❖ Become extremely cautious not to dwell on opinions - facts only matter.
- ❖ Stay hopeful; the ball is in your court.
- ❖ Do not be hard on yourself. You deserve time to heal.

CHAPTER 4

SHUT OUT THE NOISE

Life had begun to quiet down. I was now able to control the continuing playback in my mind. No more visualizing nor analyzing the pain I was feeling. I was making a conscious decision to demand my healing. It was a high priority and mandatory to continue my morning routine. I posted a YOU GOT THIS note as a reminder that I was more than determined to get back into the swing of life.

I even created a new list that I was fully committed to achieving.

One by one, I was able to cross off an accomplishment because I could simply see the goal. I was fully persuaded that what I desired to do in life would come to pass. I believed without doubting or worrying about how.

Healing seemed to be at my fingertips. *Stay focused on you, LaShawn. Your life is about you, so don't make it your concern as to how your betrayers choose to live life. It's not your concern! I mean, really, LaShawn. It's not your concern!*

Yes, I convinced my entire being that I would fully heal and that there would not be one broken piece I did not use to rebuild my life. I knew if I did not fully heal that the vision of my future would have been distorted.

I then gathered what was once considered broken pieces and wrote the remainder of my vision.

You got it; write it down and make it plain.

I can remember pondering on a few verses from the Bible, Habakkuk 2:2-3, "And the Lord answered me, and said, Write the vision, and make it plain upon tables, that he may run that readeth it. For the vision is yet for an appointed time, but at the end, it shall speak, and not lie: though it tarry, wait for it; because it will surely come, it will not tarry."

Seek And You Will Find

Healing, where have you been?

I have been waiting for you.

Thinking, dreaming, and imagining your arrival.

Healing, where are you?

I am beginning to wonder if you ever existed.

Are you just a fragment of what I desired?

No matter what I feel, I will continue to search for you.

You seem so distant.

My heart yarns for you. My soul cries out to my spirit for you.

Healing, don't you see I am in desperate need of your presence?

As I breathe, I concentrate on inhaling as well as exhaling.

But the absence of healing began to take a toil on my very being.

My existence is at stake. I am exhausted, depleted, and fragile.

Healing, where are you?

Healing, is that you?

Are you in the sound of the rain pounding on the window?

Are you in the wind that so often dried my tears?

Maybe you are in the sound of music that somehow calmed my soul.

Healing, is that you?

Were you here all the time?

Were you in the peace that allowed my eyes to close in the late night hours? Were you the memories that represented good times?

Were you the small, still voice telling me not to give up?

Maybe you were the extended arms that held me together.

Healing, could this have been you?

Healing, were you here all the time?

I often wondered how I missed your signs.

Now I know!

Oh, healing, I am convinced this must be you.

It is my pleasure to finally meet you again. Allow me to reintroduce myself.

I am that soul that cried for help, the eyes that saw but couldn't see. I am the heart that loved but still seemed to have lost. I am the one who called for you!

Thank you for answering. I am now striving to become whole.

I am living life because I owe it to you, healing.

I owe it to myself.

I am freely ending my relationship with pain.

I have finished this chapter of the book.

Stay tuned to the new series of living.

Healing brings about freedom.

Review Points

- ❖ Take control of your thoughts. Allow yourself to find peace.

- ❖ Realize life will look different, so set and accomplish goals for your life.

- ❖ Purposely develop a routine that will keep you focused while you are healing.

- ❖ Life is about you; don't concern yourself with who hurt you.

- ❖ Write your vision without any distortions, believe the vision, and work toward your vision coming to pass.

CHAPTER 5

UNDERCOVER FEAR

My former spouse and I divorced in April 2021. It was September 2021, and I believe I had just about fully healed. Certain things just didn't bother me anymore. I was enjoying exploring life. I had begun to remodel the house, which also included removing all things that represented past memories, good or not-so-good. I was feeling a little accomplished. Holidays, birthdays, and anniversaries came and left. I had no worries or no tears.

Oh, but remember, I threw the last draw four, so I was at ease. When I least expected to have a human moment, a trigger was hit. I panicked; this situation did not pan out as I had envisioned. I felt overwhelmed, stuck, and helpless. To this day, I don't know why, but I reached out to a few people trying to get someone, and I mean anyone, to assist me in taking care of some unfinished business. Needless to say, reaching out was a dead end. I quickly deleted contacts and numbers; therefore, if other triggers were exposed, I would not have the resources to reach out to the past. I would be forced to deal with myself and the present.

As I began to think rationally, I reached out to my spiritual covering, which helped calm my spirit.

Listen, I had begun to experience regrouping at its finest. I was so desperate to heal, not knowing I covered up a few leftover hurt areas. Push pause. Did I mention fear?

Well, fear can be a crippling hindrance. Fear comes in many different forms and will appear at the most inconvenient time. Fear has a way of detouring one's path.

It was frightening as I sat and thought about my age (51) and starting parts of life over. I was fearful of the unknown. I had concerns about the fear of what if and the fear of how I would not only pick up the broken pieces but how I would reconstruct them entirely. But looking back, I must admit my will to live a new life was so much more powerful than fear.

I was allowing my mind to wonder about too many things at once. It was becoming overwhelming. I was trying to seek out situations that I really had not completely allowed myself to comprehend. But that's a part of life; I knew decisions had to be made.

I began to tell myself, "Come on, LaShawn, pursue, don't procrastinate."

I had a general idea of how and what I wanted my new life to represent. I definitely set my mind on fast-forward and not rewind. I entertained absolutely nothing from the past. However, every time I pushed forward, I honestly felt fear chasing me to remind me of past situations and questioning me as to what and how I was going to do what I had imagined. Fear constantly told me I didn't have time to regroup or reframe my life. It was as if fear knew me. Fear knew all the right questions to make me pause, overthink, and analyze what I thought were my final decisions.

Fear Of?

Fear, I sincerely thought I was over you. I left you in the past. I clearly remember when I was a child being adamant about dismissing you from my presence. How dare you; you have no right.

Wait what? You laid dormant.

Fear you waited until the perfect opportunity to present yourself.

You waited all this time?

Fear, answer me!

Why?

Fear answers me!

I (fear) am here to hinder and distort your vision.

You must realize that I (fear) am only a fragment of your imagination.

I only dwell in your soul.

I (fear) only exist when you grant me access to your life.

I (fear) become stronger and powerful because of you.

What do you mean because of me?

Yes, you are responsible for my strength.

You chose to detour instead of pause.

Now you are unfamiliar with your surroundings.

Life looks different from what you had imagined.

You begin to imagine, what if I don't heal?

You imagined what if it takes longer than I expected to regroup?

What if I do not accomplish the things I desire?

What if God does not answer my prayers?

What if…..? What if……?

You see, your what ifs were interpreted as doubt.

You second-guessed your vision.

And yes, doubt opened the door for me (fear) to start off where you left me,

that is in your imagination. I used you to hinder you.

Now that you are aware of my presence, you may dismiss me at any given time However, I must admit I (fear) have enjoyed my journey with you.

I (fear) now must move on to the next hurt person.

Remember, if you slip, I (fear) will be waiting to catch you.

Sincerely fear of the past, present, and future.

Listen, the revolving door of fear had to be closed. I began to ask myself was it fear alone or was there another entity that decided to accompany fear. Oh, now life was really starting to get real. I evaluated my feelings, emotions, thought patterns, and a few other areas. However, I totally neglected a major part of healing. Perhaps the final piece to the puzzle.

Forgiveness. If I was going to build a new life, a pure heart and motive were necessary. You got it, a clean canvas! Therefore, no traces of unforgiveness could be present. I knew not only did I need to continue to be totally honest with myself, but forgiving would require more than replaying the past year over in my head and saying to myself you are no longer mad. Nope, this release was rooted a little deeper than I wanted to admit.

I am talking about 12 years of building and sharing my life with someone. Twelve years of allowing someone in the most intimate areas of my being.

Secrets shared, tears cried, and laughter that could never be measured. But nevertheless, I knew what I thought at the time would be impossible needed to be done. I knew without a second thought that forgiveness would allow me total access to what was stopping me from pursuing the future that awaited me. I proceeded with caution and prepared for the final detox.

Review Points

- ❖ Do not allow fear to control you or your decisions.
- ❖ Recognize any missed triggers and deal with them immediately.
- ❖ Don't make a cycle of repeating the past.
- ❖ The past doesn't control your future.
- ❖ Prepare for the steps in healing and life.

Chapter 6

THE FINAL DETOX

It was now December 1, 2021, and I didn't want another calendar year to pass without dealing with this heart issue. For all my Bible believers and readers, we know some things only come out through prayer and fasting. To me, fasting was the obvious thing to do. And not to mention, I was physically tired but mentally and spiritually ready to be totally free.

I had been studying and teaching the book of Daniel; therefore, a 21-day water fast seemed to be fitting. I am not suggesting that you fast, but I felt a fast was right for me. And besides, I wanted to have full control over my flesh. So, I inflicted my soul and commanded it to withhold from food.

I knew the first three days would be challenging. I kept thinking, *just get through these first days, and the hunger will go away*.

LaShawn, just stay focused on the overall task. It was now day eight, and the hunger pains were non-existent. However, a weak, queasy feeling was very much present.

I was a little concerned with my immune system weakening, so I juiced an orange on day eleven to get a little vitamin C in my body. Come on now! I wasn't not living under a rock. Wisdom would say Covid-19 was still somewhere out there. I wanted to ensure I stayed completely healthy.

On day fifteen, I had no shady ill feelings toward anyone. I prayed daily and included a prayer for the individuals I felt betrayed me. I allowed myself not to be judgmental but just to pray. It was evident that I couldn't fully heal myself, so I completely surrendered the pain while opening my heart and asking God for forgiveness for anything I had done that did not please Him. I asked God to reveal any iniquities I may have unknowingly harbored in my heart. Therefore, I used the Bible to reflect on Psalm 51 as a scripture reference for cleansing my heart.

Also, Matthew 6:9-13 provided clear instructions for forgiveness, specifically verse 12. "After this manner, therefore, pray ye: Our father which art in heaven, Hallowed be thy name. Thy Kingdom come. Thy will be done in earth as it is in heaven. Give us this day our daily bread. And forgive us our debts as we forgive our debtors. And lead us not into temptations, but deliver us from evil: For thine is the Kingdom, and the power, and the glory, forever. Amen."

At this point, I felt I was commanded to forgive. Forgiveness is the only way to move on freely in life. Total forgiveness allowed me to look at things differently. I still didn't think things were done appropriately, but at this point, what was done was over, and it was no longer my concern.

During the last six days of the fast, I thanked God for giving me a clean and forgiving heart.

My life is no longer how I knew it. Life is completely based on how I will reframe and recreate it. I decided to add an abundant amount of joy and peace while experiencing a little of the unknown.

Unforgiveness and fear will no longer manipulate the choices and decisions I make. All is forgiven!

Although I had completely forgiven and chosen not to allow fear to run my life, I felt extremely guarded. I found myself in a bubble of limitless possibilities. I constantly felt as if I was suffocating, breathless, and gasping for air. My very being was in jeopardy of not fully transitioning to my new reality. Although I confessed freedom, I didn't feel free. I had become suspicious of everyone and everything. Remember, for an entire year, I was off-grid and only accessible to very few people. I guess I had developed my own sense of protection from the world. I had been so closed off that when new came, I had questions. What are their motives? Do these people have pure hearts? Are they genuine towards me? Do they know something I don't know? Wait, I totally forgot I prayed and asked God to surround me with pure-hearted people. People who had my best interest. Friends, who I could talk to, and they could talk to me. Friends who came with positive vibes. Vibes of peace and comfort. Vibes of watching the sunset and looking forward to new, vibrant experiences. Vibes that filled the atmosphere with laughter. Vibes that could not deny the true essence of life. Vibes that bring the fragrance and aroma of liberty. Vibes that allow room for growth. Positive vibes that allow one to reap what they have sown.

I thought to myself, *you have sown some good seeds. It's now okay to let your guard down and trust. You must be open and free to reap your harvest.*

Guarded

*Here I am, confined to the season of trying not to repeat the past cycles that forced me to learn lessons that I didn't even know existed. Listening to my thoughts and convincing myself that I would never experience not living life in the moment. Moments that would pass in the blink of an eye. I found the moments somehow turned into days, weeks, and months of not fully living. I somehow built a wall around myself. I carried an invisible shield attached to a promise. A promise that I would never allow myself to feel so deeply embedded in hurt. I thought to myself, could I have been the accomplice to hurt? I had become so obsessed with protecting myself that I didn't realize I had become guarded. I blocked out people, certain places, and events. I was limiting myself. I needed help! Help trusting again and letting my guard down. Help! I was crying out. I felt my soul trapped in anguish. I wrestled with my thoughts and past experiences. In my conscience was stored a book of memories that triggered pain. I tossed and turned, seeking comfort. My spirit led me to a familiar Bible passage, Psalm 91. I felt instantly at peace. I dwelt in the secret place of the Most High & abided in the shadows of the Almighty. God was and is my refuge, fortress, and strong tower. In God, I trust. My trust in God slowly allowed me to lower my guard. I removed the invisible shield that no one seemed to notice but me.
In my heart and soul, I finally knew I would be okay. I now believe my protection is a shared responsibility. My guardian angels have taken charge all about me. There was and is a divine hedge of protection that had been placed around me. Selah- stop, pause & think about it.*

I am now willing to give living life my all!

Dominate the day, conquer what comes your way, and subdue it - make lower in rank anything that attempts to make you ponder on the past.

So be it!

Wow, just like that, I felt free; every trace of pain, hurt, burden, betrayal, and ill feelings vanished.

I mean, it really wasn't just like that. I put in the work. I grinded for myself, and I am proud of myself. The past year and a half could have easily broken, killed, or destroyed me. But I refused to be defeated.

To my surprise, people began to reach out and express that they were rooting for me. They sent social media messages stating they were glad to see God kept His hand upon me.

It was funny because I never used social media as a place to vent, but needless to say, others did. This allowed many mutual associates to have a general idea of what happened. But, I just commented thank you and kept living.

I knew without any doubt that God was and is definitely a promise keeper. He is the same yesterday, today, and forever. Despite what happens in life, His promises are yes and amen.

I continued to teach with confidence every Sunday to a small group of women. I sought God concerning each teaching. I made sure I never forced my opinion or hurt upon them. I refused to bleed pain on others. So, as I received the word of God attached with instructions, I ministered with grace what was given to me by the Holy Spirit. I poured into the group as they received. We all trusted God, and He delivered. Everyday life skills and experiences wrapped around His word allowed us to live according to what was designed to push us into our destiny with purpose.

I am because God is ………….

Review Points

- ❖ Listen. Allow the spirit within to lead you to total freedom.

- ❖ Realize that healing is more about you than what happened to you.

- ❖ It is in your best interest to totally forgive and not concern yourself with the past.

- ❖ There is a different perspective than how you saw it in the beginning.

CHAPTER 7

ALL IS FORGIVEN

The dictionary defines forgive as to grant a pardon for or remission of an offense, debt, or absolves. To cease from feeling resentment (Merriam-Webster.com, 2023).

Resentment - to show displeasure or indignation at some act, remark, or person regarded as causing injury or insult (Merriam-Webster.com, 2023).

I now can honestly say that I finally understand the statement that forgiveness is not for the other person; it's for you. Note to self: Got it! I was no longer upset or disappointed in my former spouse or the marital affair. I wasn't even mad at the way it happened. I just knew without a doubt that I made the correct decision to let go of any and everything from my past experience. I really allowed myself to comprehend a different perspective. I often thought of the past mental state of my betrayer. Just maybe they thought their actions were the only way to end the marriage without any explanation. Maybe it was what they thought was the master plan to obtain a new life, a new love, and a new family. Maybe in their mind, they saw no way to explain the loss of love they had for me and the growing apart that had occurred. Maybe they didn't want to feel like they were a failure. Whatever their perspective, I am now grateful that God allowed me another opportunity to live a new life despite the pain. I continue asking myself how many people I know have been granted another opportunity to live freely. I have been granted a variety of options for my future. The first option was to tell my story to help others emotionally heal from life. Healing is great, yet underrated. Sometimes society labels the act of healing as being negative. It simply means to realign, adjust what was broken, mend, repair, and to be peaceful and happy.

A Letter To My Betrayal

I didn't understand. I couldn't comprehend. I was so in denial that I would not even allow myself to believe the reality of emotions and feelings I was dealing with. It was like a nightmare that I experienced every day for at least four months to one year. The disbelief became overwhelming. I tried not to imagine the very act that led to the betrayal. I tried to pray the betrayal away. I even tried to live over the betrayal. But the betrayal was there and not willing to go away. Betrayal & the betrayer stayed in my face. It was clear, and I had to accept the fact that I underestimated the trust, the loyalty, and even the respect I thought we had established together. I found myself in a place where, time and time again, I continued to tell myself I thought so much more of you, the betrayer. I was so disappointed that I had no words to express the hurt and pain I was feeling. My trust, hope, and expectations of you have been shattered. Day after day, I carried around a sense of lost hope. I prayed until I had no energy. I cried until I was exhausted. And then I realized the betrayer was trying to live up to a standard that, in their own strength, they were not capable of accomplishing. The betrayer was hiding fears, disappointments, pain, dramatic experiences, trauma and all of their unsettled childhood memories. The betrayer is just someone who has been living two lives. The life full of false realities, unaccomplished goals, and dreams but yet trying to display success.

Then there was the reality of wanting deliverance as well as wanting to be free from the person society allowed them to create. The betrayer just wanted something new. New will come when one does not repeat the old.

To my betrayer, I am healing daily. I have forgiven you for not knowing the hope, trust, and expectations I had placed upon you. I have forgiven myself for having too much trust in man. I know, as I should have from the beginning, to place all my hope and trust in God. I can truly say if God had taken His hand off of me, I would not have made it. So, to my betrayer, thank you because if you had not betrayed me, I would not have an opportunity to live a new, amazing life. I live my life like there is no tomorrow. I live with no regrets. There is no compromising. Finally, to betrayer, I understand you simply did what you thought was best to experience a different life. It was unfortunate that your actions were at my expense. Thank you again; through this experience, I have grown, and I appreciate the new life God is allowing me to live.

I say love is God-ordained, and I shall love again.

#fatherknowsbest

#loveagain

#loveisgodordained

#healingisgoodforthesoul

#iamagoodthing

#prophetesslashawn

#brokenpiecesmaketheperfectbuildingblocks

Review Points

- ❖ Forgiveness is really for you.
- ❖ Having a different perspective doesn't mean you agree with what occurred.
- ❖ Healing is a positive attribute of your life.
- ❖ Hold nothing back by expressing yourself and finally embracing new opportunities in life.

CHAPTER 8

COMPLETION – NO EXPECTATIONS OF MAN

I had finally ended the last twelve years with peace. The last chapters of my former life were completely over. It was now time to transition without any expectation of other people. I created a bucket list of things I wanted to experience in life. I desired to live freely without any restraints. This meant positioning myself in a totally different environment. Over the past year or two, I allowed myself to have a totally different outlook on life. What used to be the center of my life no longer received attention. Things that I used to deem important were no longer of interest to me.

In my spirit, I knew the time was near for me to branch out again into full entrepreneurship. I wasn't quite sure when, but I had an urge. So, I cleaned my work office, leaving only the necessary materials to function daily. I began strategically putting a plan in place to manage the corporate salon back to the top of the District. After this was accomplished, I would then make my departure. I strongly believe what one sows is what one will reap. Therefore, this was the perfect plan. I would surely reap great things in my personal business for ensuring I managed the corporate salon well.

I hired a few more stylists, ensuring the controllable profits would surpass the salon expenses. The salon retail and services were excelling beyond plan. The back bar inventory was increased, and at this point, the salon had coverage every minute of the hour. Everything was set in place and rapidly moving forward.

The progress of the salon allowed me to take a small break to attend my niece's wedding in Philly. I had not serviced a bride in years, which really brought back good memories.

I held on to those memories as I returned to work and continued following the original plan.

A few weeks later, the new G.M. informed me that my work was impeccable, but they believed I had violated a policy thirty days ago. To my surprise, I was not aware of the policy they were referring to. I had been employed there for five years and eight months; therefore, I knew the policies and procedures. To this day, that policy still has not been fully found. I stated the policy back to corporate, but they decided to allow the G.M. to terminate my employment with the company.

I guess my end came sooner than I planned. I looked at it as if God decided to tweak my plan. And that was absolutely fine with me. I trusted God, and at this point in life, I did not have any expectations of people, so I knew God couldn't make any mistakes. And besides, I still had a few broken pieces that needed to be put in their proper places.

Although I did find it funny that this all happened one day before my 52nd birthday. Happy birthday to me. Talk about reinventing life.

I had been scheduled to take a permanent makeup class that weekend. So, you see, I had no time to stop or worry. This was all a part of God's plan to allow me to better myself. I was learning to accept my new life. However, I was a little disappointed that the corporate office didn't give me a verbal or written warning. Nevertheless, I was determined to push through life with an attitude of gratefulness.

I enjoyed my time with the company, but it was now time to focus on myself and business.

The next few months, I vacationed with my family and took a few more out-of-state advance permanent tattoo brow, henna, tint, and lamination classes.

I managed things one day at a time, promising myself to enjoy every moment of life. I am fully convinced that the Bible is definitely correct. All things work together for the good of them that are called according to His purpose. I just followed directions, wrote the plan, and made it plain. It was God who brought it to pass. This was one of those situations where I would honestly say I was thankful the manifestation wasn't according to my timing. If God had not stepped in, I probably would have missed my opportunity of departure. I would have been putting my all into the corporate salon when the organization just wants its business to operate according to the profit and operating statements set every fiscal year.

I was and still am to this day grateful for God tweaking my plan. Actually, grateful is an understatement. I realized what appeared not to be a good situation actually was what I needed to dedicate time freely to developing my second business, LaBella Bridal and Brows. I have learned at times when things seem not to be as good, never refer to them as bad because somehow better has been destined to show itself; and of course, there is a learning experience. I simply allowed myself to be open and recognize the options that life presents. Life is going to be what I make it.

No Expectations

Expectations of man are a mere image of yesterday.

Yesterday has passed, tomorrow has not yet come.

The present is a moment. A moment is a minute.

A minute to make a decision to meet the image I imagined of you.

You used to cry, but now you laugh.

You value every moment in time.

You allow life to experience you.

You experience life with no chains and no strings.

In other words, no restraints or no limitations on my expectations of you.

You are me. Me, myself, and I.

My present is my future. My future is me.

I am me, fearfully and wonderfully made.

God has plans that He thinks toward me. Plans of good and not of evil.

Plans that will bring to an expected ending.

Review Points

- ❖ Peacefully close old chapters.
- ❖ Do not put any expectations on people.
- ❖ Life plans may change, but go with the flow.
- ❖ There is no such thing as a bad day.
- ❖ Allow your creative side to produce new inner desires.
- ❖ Boldly pursue life and new business adventures.
- ❖ Always display gratitude.

CHAPTER 9
TRY NEW THINGS

Now that I was no longer a helpmate nor a corporate salon manager, opportunity presented itself for me to explore my secret heart's desires. Although I was great at what I did, the season of expecting to support someone else's dreams, goals, visions, or assignments was over. It was time for my heart's desires to become realities. I felt the time was at hand to share my story, and as I healed, I made notations of my steps and progress. So, why not share?

Being an author was one of my desires, but I often thought about what topics to write about.

I have learned over the years that God doesn't waste time or things. God turned my not-so-great experiences around for my good. I now speak on what was because I realize that somewhere out there is someone whose life is being interrupted by someone's lack of concern for the consequences of their actions.

As I write and others read, there is a person who is devastated by someone else's behavior. There is a man, a woman, and even a child thinking why and trying to put together shattered pieces of their lives.

Don't fret on the other side of what appears to be an unfortunate circumstance. There is always an opportunity for better. Stay the course and run the race because, eventually, time will expire for what caused distress in one's life. Clear visions will appear for constructing the broken pieces into a perfect building block of success.

Speaking of building blocks, I decided to tackle a few things on my bucket list.

I wanted to meet new people and experience different things, but I didn't quite know what. I was convinced I would know when different things came across my path. One day, I logged into I.G. and saw an ad for an introduction class to Pilates. And with just a simple click of a button, there different was inviting me to engage in a new adventure.

I faithfully attended Pilates three days a week for the next seven months. Surprisingly, Pilates was more than just reforming and stretching my body. Pilates was a meeting place for people from all walks of life. I quickly became accustomed to normalizing in the same room all generations doing the same thing but for different reasons. Baby Boomers, GenX, Millennials, and a few GenZ. We all allowed Pilates to become a place where we relearned how to relax our minds and focus on the present moment.

Pilates forced me to be aware of my breathing and body. The practice of Pilates taught me not to allow room for tension or stress but to reform, regroup, and obtain strength.

Strangely relaxing and deep breathing contribute to my being able to clear my mind while enhancing my meditation with God. It felt good that my mind was not oversaturated with the everyday hustle of life. I pondered one thing at a time. Each day was something different. Sunday, I may have meditated on the marvelous works of God, and by Wednesday, I was visualizing traveling the world.

Traveling always seems to be a great idea, so I added a few countries and states to my bucket list. I even made a new visual board. This time, I was happy to say it wasn't a healing board.

New Things

Make new friends but keep the old. One is silver, and the other is gold.

Old things are like silver, having value but just not enough to compete with the new. New things are just like gold lying on an island tucked away in a chest with treasures unknown. Access to unlimited gold but hesitant to reach for the stars. Adventures ahead of uncharted territory, unknown spheres, rocky roads & untamed seas cause one to retreat to the old, familiar & comfortable. A loud voice demands to press toward what is new. The voice realizes pressing holds an internal purpose that new has never seen, felt, or conquered.

New has nothing to lose and deserves the experience.

New will never know what was nor is to come until a chance has been taken on something new, a chance on YOU.

Review Points

- ❖ Do not take responsibility for someone else's goals, dreams, and visions.
- ❖ Continue to focus on you; all things will work out for your good.
- ❖ Lessons taught also come in the form of disappointments.
- ❖ It's okay to share your healing experience with others who may be hurting.
- ❖ Try new things.
- ❖ Create a new bucket list or vision board.

CHAPTER 10

HAPPINESS IS PRICELESS

According to the English dictionary, happiness is the quality or state of being happy. It is good fortune, pleasure, contentment, and joy (Merriam-Webster.com, 2023).

Now that happiness has been defined, there is absolutely no reason to take being happy for granted. Good fortune, pleasure, contentment, and joy are necessary and extremely valuable.

Happiness is beyond any price someone could offer to pay. It is an asset in life that many people undervalue. Most people rely on their significant other to make them happy. Others seek out relatives and close friends for feelings of joy or delight. However, if happiness does not come from within, there will be a void and displeasure with all that one has surrounded oneself with.

I fully believe everyone is responsible for their own happiness. Placing this burden on others is entirely too much for them to bear. One will become exhausted trying to make others happy. I am not saying that someone cannot be included in one's life and both receive happiness because of each other's presence. I am just saying taking authority over one's own happiness directs one to a clear vision of one's life.

With happiness in mind, I ensured I did things that interested me. I planned dinners, outings, workout sessions, movie nights, business events, turn-around trips, and other things that brought me joy. I refused to do things that I didn't want to do. I was determined to make the best of my life. I believed each day there should be some type of fulfillment. Somedays, I didn't go out; I just sat and talked to God, and other days, I listened.

God and I had conversations concerning what I had dreamed the night before, visions, and, of course, assignments. The conversations gave me directions on my next move and reassured confidence that God always has my best interest.

I was interested in learning a new language and becoming a better swimmer. I know a few words in Spanish, but not enough to have a conversation. I could thread water and doggy paddle, but this was far from swimming. I sought out a few classes, but they interfered with my schedule. However, they are on my bucket list. Oh, and I also want to learn a few ballroom dances. God help! Rhythm skipped over me at birth!

Happiness

Happiness is that desire, feeling, and excitement that causes the heart to pound. Happiness is a dream that manifests naturally. It is peace surrounding the sight of the clouds. Happiness exposes joy. Joy captivates the sight of visions dancing and singing in the wind. The wind signals the rain to pour a shower of blessings that are unnumbered. Angelic beings begin to rapidly move throughout the earth realm to fulfill the final destination of the outpouring of blessings.

In the right place at the right time, good things have fallen on those who believed. Very few invited happiness and joy to have a permanent place in their lives. These few knew to make happiness a part of everyday life because everyday life is depending on them; life is depending on you.

Review Points

- ❖ Do not devalue your happiness.
- ❖ You decide your happiness. Don't depend on others to make you happy.
- ❖ Do what brings you joy.
- ❖ Surround yourself with like-minded people.

CHAPTER 11

LOVE AGAIN

Love - to have a strong liking for; to take pleasure in (Merriam-Webster.com, 2023).

Google the word love; some articles say there are four types of love: Storge, Agape, Philia, and Eros. Other articles will say that there are eight types of love, adding Pragma, Ludus, Mania, and Philautia.

I strongly believe everyone has an opinion of what love is. Their answer will probably be based on their past experiences. Some will reminisce on how someone made them feel. Others will associate love with words of affirmation and affection. Very few will answer according to how they treat and view themselves.

It became a must that I continue to stay focused on myself. I rarely concerned myself with feelings of the past. I treated myself exceptionally well and never allowed anyone or anything the opportunity to pull me from the love I had for myself.

I have come to understand that one must wholeheartedly love oneself before fully extending love to others.

Sometimes, we as people take for granted or assume others love themselves. Most people cover up what they perceive as flaws. They try to change what they don't like and never truly love themselves. People base love on what society has forced upon them and deems acceptable.

I am not saying do not work to better yourself. I am simply saying do not make that one unique thing about you a flaw.

I have flaws, but I have learned not to base my love for myself on them or someone else's opinion concerning me. Others' opinions are not facts; they can be an open doorway to love or not to love oneself.

I really do what makes me happy without hurting others. Being happy helps me develop a strong liking and take pleasure in those I have spent time with. And since I have been focusing on reinventing myself, I have adapted to loving myself even more than before. The healed me has introduced me to me. I can now remove the lock from my heart and freely love without worrying about a not-so-perfect me. Since starting my healing journey, I have always stopped to notice and acknowledge how far I have come. I continue to love myself while implementing small things I desire to enhance in different areas.

Now, for the most part, I often shy away from the risk of opening my heart and inviting love from others. I constantly tell myself not to become closed off because I believe everyone has the right to love and be loved. I often pray that I attract those who know how to give and receive love. I was very strategic in my healing; therefore, I am aware of love, red flags, and warning signs. Until love arrives, I guess it will just be God, family, football ("Best Man Holiday.") (Lol, I am just kidding. I told you all I love movies.) Listen, laughing and not being angry concerning the past is a win for me.

Love is God-Ordained

Long walks on the beach, only stopping to watch the sunset. Early morning laughter as we stare in amazement while the sun once again takes its rightful place and allows the moon to rest. Dancing to the melody of smooth sounds that only two can hear. Listening to the whispers of peace while feeling refreshed as love approaches our hearts. Glazing into the eyes of the one who understands and appreciates your presence. Both pinching ourselves to ensure we are not trapped in dreamland. Taking a deep breath, thanking the Creator of love for allowing two pure souls to find each other. Some would call it a fantasy. Some would say it is not reality. Some would even question the mere facts that are evident. I would simply call it an answered prayer. Together, we took advantage of the opportunity to love and receive love in return. I like to believe God has released a few of my bottled tears and converted them into love. Thy is Love, and love has found thee.

Review Points

- ❖ Love yourself before you offer your love to others.
- ❖ Don't be fearful. It's okay to open your heart to receive love.
- ❖ Have a clear understanding of what you perceive as love.
- ❖ You deserve to love again.

Thank you. I pray grace, healing, and peace for you!

The following section is your building blocks planner. Always remember it's imperative to maintain your new way of living. *Building Blocks Planner* will meet your needs, whether business, things to do, or even saving money.

Congratulations, new is at your fingertips!

TRENDY & PRAIZEY BUILDING BLOCKS PLANNER

Curated by LaShawn Walker

Trendy & Praizey's Pledge

"For Thy art the maker of the heavens and the earth,
Thy knoweth all things,
Thy keepeth me from thy enemy and thyself,
Fear is my past,
Honesty and truth are my present,
Freedom is my future,
Together they are the promises I hold in my heart,
The dreams I vision,
The realities I accept,
The path I choose to travel,
The designation, the journey, the arrival,
The freedom-,
Freedom Selah- stop, pause & and think about,
Freedom" *Prophetess LaShawn Walker*

Great Job!

Way to plan. You decided to launch out into the deep. You won't sink. Relax. Imagine your journey of releasing, regrouping, & reforming your life.

Dream and dream big. Again, I say relax. Dreams are internal realities waiting to be free. You owe it to yourself to have freedom. Freedom is simply being who God called you to be. You were fearfully and wonderfully made. To be whole and complete. To love and to be loved. To also be stylish and spiritual. To be saved and on-trend. Well, that just about sums it up.

OH NO, wait, don't forget your stash cash! We must be good stewards of finances.

Selah,

Prophetess LaShawn Walker

January

MON	TUE	WED	THU	FRI	SAT	SUN

MONTH'S VISION

DUE DATE: _____

☐ ACCOMPLISHED   ☐ CONTINUATION

"Broken pieces make
the perfect
building blocks"
#pickupthepieces
#ProphetessLaShawn

Business Tools

IDEAS

MONEY MOVES

RESOURCES

DEUTERONOMY 8:18 "BUT THOU SHALT REMEMBER THE LORD THY GOD WHO GIVES YOU THE POWER TO GAIN WEALTH."

Things To Remember

notes

February

MON	TUE	WED	THU	FRI	SAT	SUN

MONTH'S VISION

DUE DATE: _____

☐ ACCOMPLISHED ☐ CONTINUATION

"Live with
no regrets"
#selflove
#selfcare

Business Tools

IDEAS

MONEY MOVES

RESOURCES

DEUTERONOMY 8:18 "BUT THOU SHALT REMEMBER THE LORD THY GOD WHO GIVES YOU THE POWER TO GAIN WEALTH."

Things To Remember

notes

March

MON	TUE	WED	THU	FRI	SAT	SUN

MONTH'S VISION

DUE DATE: _____

☐ ACCOMPLISHED   ☐ CONTINUATION

"Position Your Self:
On you mark,
get Set,
SOAR!!!"
#EaglesFlyHigh

Business Tools

IDEAS

MONEY MOVES

RESOURCES

DEUTERONOMY 8:18 "BUT THOU SHALT REMEMBER THE LORD THY GOD WHO GIVES YOU THE POWER TO GAIN WEALTH."

Things To Remember

notes

April

MON	TUE	WED	THU	FRI	SAT	SUN

MONTH'S VISION

DUE DATE: _____

☐ ACCOMPLISHED   ☐ CONTINUATION

"Small accomplishment, small acknowledgment! Big Accomplishment, big reward! #NewChapter #NewBook

Business Tools

IDEAS	MONEY MOVES

RESOURCES

DEUTERONOMY 8:18 "BUT THOU SHALT REMEMBER THE LORD THY GOD WHO GIVES YOU THE POWER TO GAIN WEALTH."

Things To Remember

notes

May

MON	TUE	WED	THU	FRI	SAT	SUN

MONTH'S VISION

DUE DATE: _____

☐ ACCOMPLISHED   ☐ CONTINUATION

"Regroup does not mean failed. My options are my choices I have chosen."
#Winning

Business Tools

IDEAS	MONEY MOVES

RESOURCES

DEUTERONOMY 8:18 "BUT THOU SHALT REMEMBER THE LORD THY GOD WHO GIVES YOU THE POWER TO GAIN WEALTH."

Things To Remember

notes

June

MON	TUE	WED	THU	FRI	SAT	SUN

MONTH'S VISION

DUE DATE: _____
☐ ACCOMPLISHED   ☐ CONTINUATION

"I determine my outcome.
My victory & success
are within my reach."
#IGotThis
#Survivor

Business Tools

IDEAS

MONEY MOVES

RESOURCES

DEUTERONOMY 8:18 "BUT THOU SHALT REMEMBER THE LORD THY GOD WHO GIVES YOU THE POWER TO GAIN WEALTH."

Things To Remember

notes

July

MON	TUE	WED	THU	FRI	SAT	SUN

MONTH'S VISION

DUE DATE: _____

☐ ACCOMPLISHED   ☐ CONTINUATION

"Unique, peculiar, different. It's not just about being different, it's about being free."
#Freedom

Business Tools

IDEAS

MONEY MOVES

RESOURCES

DEUTERONOMY 8:18 "BUT THOU SHALT REMEMBER THE LORD THY GOD WHO GIVES YOU THE POWER TO GAIN WEALTH."

Things To Remember

notes

August

	MON	TUE	WED	THU	FRI	SAT	SUN

MONTH'S VISION

DUE DATE: _____

☐ ACCOMPLISHED   ☐ CONTINUATION

"I must find peace in the midst of chaos."
#SilenceTheNoise
#MeditationOnPurpose

Business Tools

IDEAS	MONEY MOVES

RESOURCES

DEUTERONOMY 8:18 "BUT THOU SHALT REMEMBER THE LORD THY GOD WHO GIVES YOU THE POWER TO GAIN WEALTH."

Things To Remember

notes

September

MON	TUE	WED	THU	FRI	SAT	SUN

MONTH'S VISION

DUE DATE: _____

☐ ACCOMPLISHED ☐ CONTINUATION

"Focus on what I want & what's to come instead of what I don't have and what's not."
#SpeakLife

Business Tools

IDEAS	MONEY MOVES

RESOURCES

DEUTERONOMY 8:18 "BUT THOU SHALT REMEMBER THE LORD THY GOD WHO GIVES YOU THE POWER TO GAIN WEALTH."

Things To Remember

notes

October

MON	TUE	WED	THU	FRI	SAT	SUN

MONTH'S VISION

DUE DATE: _____

☐ ACCOMPLISHED   ☐ CONTINUATION

"Change is a good thing.
Adjust, not compromise."
#Mindset
#ThinkOnNewThings
#DoSomethingDifferent

Business Tools

IDEAS	MONEY MOVES

RESOURCES

DEUTERONOMY 8:18 "BUT THOU SHALT REMEMBER THE LORD THY GOD WHO GIVES YOU THE POWER TO GAIN WEALTH."

Things To Remember

notes

November

MON	TUE	WED	THU	FRI	SAT	SUN

MONTH'S VISION

DUE DATE: _____

☐ ACCOMPLISHED   ☐ CONTINUATION

"Reformed. Released. Regrouped.
No resentment."
#Love
#LiveLife
#ItWasWorthIt

Business Tools

IDEAS	MONEY MOVES

RESOURCES

DEUTERONOMY 8:18 "BUT THOU SHALT REMEMBER THE LORD THY GOD WHO GIVES YOU THE POWER TO GAIN WEALTH."

Things To Remember

notes

December

MON	TUE	WED	THU	FRI	SAT	SUN

MONTH'S VISION

DUE DATE: _____

☐ ACCOMPLISHED ☐ CONTINUATION

"Eleven + One =
Make Life Count
#MissionAccomplished
#Changed
#TrendyandPraizey

Business Tools

IDEAS	MONEY MOVES

RESOURCES

DEUTERONOMY 8:18 "BUT THOU SHALT REMEMBER THE LORD THY GOD WHO GIVES YOU THE POWER TO GAIN WEALTH."

Things To Remember

notes

ABOUT THE AUTHOR

LASHAWN WALKER

I am who I am. I am fearfully and wonderfully made. I am a Washingtonian, born and raised in the Nation's Capital. One of God's creations. A spiritual and honest being. I am aware of my purpose and existence. I am honored and grateful to share wisdom, knowledge, and love.

I am peace to many and joy to others. I am just me. A Prophetess called and chosen by God. I am mostly happy and sometimes playful. When I am tired, I can be funny yet extremely mellow. When serious, I am extremely professional. I am the owner of Trendy & Praizey, LLC (Spiritual & Retail Therapy) and a Manager of a six-figure Corporate Salon.

Yes, this is me. This is my life, and I love living it!

For more information about me, visit www.trendyandpraizey.com.

REFERENCES

Forgive. (2023). *Merriam-Webster*. Retrieved May 31, 2023 from https://www.merriam-webster.com/dictionary/forgive

Resentment. (2023). *Merriam-Webster*. Retrieved May 31, 2023 from https://www.merriam-webster.com/dictionary/resentment

Happiness. (2023). *Merriam-Webster*. Retrieved May 31, 2023 from https://www.merriam-webster.com/dictionary/happiness

Love. (2023). *Merriam-Webster*. Retrieved May 31, 2023 from https://www.merriam-webster.com/dictionary/love

www.ingramcontent.com/pod-product-compliance
Lightning Source LLC
Chambersburg PA
CBHW061403010526
44119CB00010B/245